UNSUNG FIGURES IN RENSSELAER, NEW YORK

CONTENTS

Unsung Figures in Rensselaer, New York

JYQUAN STEWART

This book is dedicated to the city of Rensselaer, New and it's contributing into National History.

| **1** |

Catherine Stewart

Catherine Stewart is an African American woman born on April 5, 1947 in Kinston, North Carolina. She grew up in a poor family and her father left when she was a very young age. Her mother was Mary Halloway of Kinston, North Carolina. In her late 20's Catherine Stewart moved to upstate New York and married Willie Stewart of Macon, Georgia. She worked as a certified nurse assistant and her husband was a college professor while also serving in the military. Catherine attended an apostolic house church called The Church of Jesus Christ Light of The World and met a woman pastor named Effie Chapman from Los Angeles, California, the wife of Elder John Chapman. Pastor Chapman preached in church, in houses, and on the streets. She preached at a revival one night with over 200 members and that night she felt God's call and felt like she was going to fly away, she said "something is going to happen and I'll be a part of it." She told the Lord I'll leave Los Angeles tonight. All she had in her pocket was $10.00 and that was for bills. She received help from the Lord and moved to Rensselaer, New York. One night in the house church Pastor Chapman was preaching on hell and The Holy Ghost knocked on the heart of Catherine Stewart with powerful conviction. Catherine Stewart knew she needed a savior for her sins. With so much conviction that night Catherine Stewart had a Bible opened and cried out to the Lord and said "I don't want to go to hell and be damned for eternity, I want to go to heaven." That night she was saved and received the Holy Ghost. Catherine Stewart's grandson wanted to preserve her legacy because it had a powerful effect on him. Catherine Stewart died on October 22, 2015.

| 2 |

Cornelius J. "Butch" Mahar, Jr.:
A Life of Service

Born in Rensselaer, New York, Cornelius J. "Butch" Mahar, Jr. is a man of unwavering dedication and resilience. Raised by Cornelius J. Mahar, Sr. and Clara B. Lord Mahar, and brother to Thomas, James, and Kathleen, Butch's journey is a testament to the power of perseverance and commitment. Butch attended St. John's Academy during his formative years and graduated from Van Rensselaer High

School in 1965. He furthered his education at Hudson Valley Community College while awaiting his entry into the Navy.

Butch's service to the country began in 1966 when he joined the US Naval Reserves. He served active duty from 1967 to 1969 in Norfolk, VA aboard the USS ORION AS-18. In the Armory, he repaired small arms for submarines and torpedoes, stood watch over nuclear warheads, and distributed ammunition and firearms to sailors. He remained in the US Naval Reserves until 1972.After his military service, Butch was employed for 37 years as a truck driver and mechanic for Polsinello Fuels. He resided in the city of Rensselaer until 2011, when he moved to East Greenbush. Butch is a Paid Up for Life member of the Gerald O' Neil Post #1683 and a Life Member of the Rensselaer Knights of Columbus, E.F. Hart Hose, and the Hendrick Hudson Fish and Game Club.

Butch's life story is powerful: the strength of character, dedication to service, and commitment to family and community. His legacy continues to inspire those who knew him and those who will come to know his story.

Picture of Queenie Holloway

| 3 |

Queenie Holloway: A Life of Service and Devotion

Queenie Holloway was born in the 1930s she was born in Kinston, North Carolina She moved to Upstate, New York in the 1960s saying that :"She would spend the rest of her life there". Her children are Jessie R. (Marie) Holloway, Marilyn Holloway (Isaiah), and Anthony Holloway. She was a member of Bethany Baptist Church in Albany, NY for over 45 years. Queenie was a faithful servant of God. She served on the usher board, scholarship committee, trustee board, deaconess board church choir and was a Mother of the church. Queenie worked at the Daughters of Sarah Nursing Home for many years. After retiring she spent most of her time enjoying family and friends. She was an avid bowler in area leagues. Mother Queenie Holloway entered into rest on July 23rd at home. Her funeral was held at the W. J. Lyons Jr. Funeral Home in Rensselaer, New York.

| 4 |

Casey Frankoski

Casey Frankoski, born on April 11, 1995, in Albany, NY, was a beacon of light known for her infectious smile and empathetic nature. Raised in East Greenbush before moving to Rensselaer, she was the beloved daughter of James and Jill (Nardacci) Frankoski. Her life, tragically cut short at the age of 28 in a helicopter accident on March 8, 2024, was marked by service, determination, and an unwavering love for her country the USA. Casey's dedication to the United States was evident in her military career. She enlisted in the Army National Guard in October 2016, rose to the rank of Chief Warrant Officer 2 by 2021, and trained to become a UH-60 Black Hawk helicopter pilot. Her service included a deployment to Kuwait from November 2018 to September 2019 with Detachment 5, Company C, 2nd Battalion,

245th Aviation Regiment as a Mission Planner. After further training in Alabama, Casey was deployed again as a pilot to Texas with the Detachment 2, Company A, 1st Battalion, 224 Aviation Regiment to patrol the United States - Mexico border on October 11, 2023. Her commendable service earned her numerous honors, including the Army Commendation Medal, Army Achievement Medal, and Basic Aviator Badge. Casey's commitment to her community was equally strong. She was a volunteer firefighter at the Best Luther Fire Department, a member of the Environmental Conservation Corp., and a current member of the American Legion Gerald O'Neil Post 1683.

Education played a significant role in Casey's life. A graduate of Columbia High School in 2013, she was a member of the Varsity Bowling team. She continued her education at Schenectady County Community College, earning an associate degree in social science and participating in the National Junior College Championship bowling team. At the time of her passing, Casey was completing her bachelor's degree in emergency management at Excelsior College.

Casey's love for the outdoors was fostered through her 13 years as a Girl Scout and her time at Camp Little Notch. She was a cheerleader for East Greenbush Pop Warner, played softball for the East Greenbush Girls Softball League, and was a dedicated member of a travel bowling league. Her passion for adventure led her to travel extensively, attending World Youth Day three times and recently traveling with her family to Alaska.

Casey is survived by her parents, her grandfather Raymond Frankoski, brothers Jesse (Reigan) Frankoski and Tyler Trembly, sisters-in-law Lindsey and Autumn, nieces and nephews Stella, Peyton, Xylas, Charlotte Trembly, Mia, and Finnley Frankoski, and her soulmate Anthony DeGregorio. She also leaves behind her three cats: Lulu, Millie, and Juju. Casey's impact on the lives of those around her was profound, and she will be sorely missed.

| 5 |

The Vanishing of Frank Connell

The mysterious disappearance of Frank Connell in 2007 had left the Rensselaer police and the local community puzzled for years. However, a decade later, a breakthrough came in the form of a skull found near the Hudson River, which was eventually identified as Connell's.

In the spring of 2007, the city of Rensselaer, New York, was gripped by a mystery that would remain unsolved for over a decade. Frank Connell, a local man known for his regular presence at the city's bars, disappeared without a trace on the night of April 20. His last known whereabouts were at Den-Den's Bar on Broadway, where he was seen leaving between 8:30 and 9 p.m. His sudden absence from his job as a drywall installer, a position he had held for 26 years, raised immediate concern. His employer and family, unable to reach him, reported him missing.

The initial investigation into Connell's disappearance yielded no substantial leads. When police visited his apartment, there was no sign of foul play or struggle. Despite rumors and speculations over the years, none could be substantiated1. There was also no indication of Connell struggling with suicidal thoughts before his disappearance, based on interviews with family and friends.

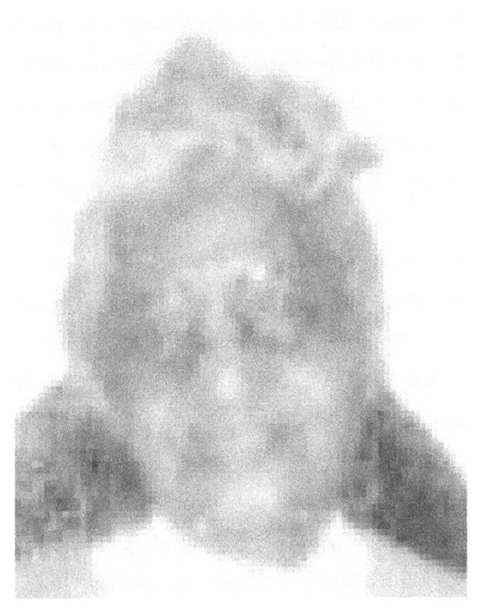

| 6 |

Pastor Effie Chapman

In the heart of Los Angeles, California, during the early 20th century, a remarkable story began to unfold. It was the life of Pastor Effie Chapman, a woman whose profound spiritual journey would leave an indelible mark. Born to Charles and Anna Holcomb, Effie's upbringing in the bustling city of Los Angeles set the stage for what would become a lifelong commitment to her faith. As a female African American Apostolic Pentecostal Holiness preacher, she broke through societal barriers with a message of Pentecost. Chapman's ministry was not confined to the walls of a church; the streets became her pulpit, homes her sanctuary, and revivals her arena. Her passionate preaching drew crowds, and her prophetic voice resonated with many, foretelling events with uncanny accuracy, including a significant earthquake in Los Angeles.

One night, she was preaching at a revival with over 200 people, but that night, that's all God wanted her there for. She felt as if she was going to fly away and say, "Something will happen, and I'll be a part of it". She told the Lord, "I'll leave Los Angeles tonight. All she had in her pocket was ten dollars and that was for the bill. Lord helped her with funds and She moved to Rensselaer, New York, where she planted the "Church of Jesus Christ Light Of The World," a house church that would become a beacon of light for many

People thought Pastor Chapman was crazy. God spoke to her and she heard him. Pastor Chapman used to see things, and God gave her visions of the future. Among them was a poignant message for the Stewart family, predicting both tribulation and divine calling. Her prophetic gift also foresaw the passing of her beloved husband, Elder John Chapman, which occurred as his favorite hymn played—a testament to her deep spiritual connection.

Introduction: City Of Rensselaer, New York

R ensselaer is a city in Rensselaer County, New York, United States, and is located on the east side of the Hudson River, directly opposite of Albany. Rensselaer is on the western border of Rensselaer County.

The region now known as Rensselaer has a rich and storied history. Initially part of the Rensselaerswyck manor, the area was established in 1630, marking the arrival of the first known European resident. The area was originally named Greenbush, a term signifying pine trees.

In 1686, the County of Albany was formed, incorporating this area within its boundaries. However, in 1791, the County of Rensselaer was carved out from Albany. In the same year, the Town of Rensselaerswyck was established, which was renamed to the Town of Greenbush in 1792.

The Village of Greenbush, nestled within the town of the same name, was officially incorporated in 1815. By 1897, Greenbush had grown significantly and was chartered as a city, adopting the name Rensselaer. The city expanded its limits in 1902 by annexing the Village of Bath on the Hudson and a portion of the western part of the town of East Greenbush.

In 1932, the Port of Rensselaer was constructed, marking a significant milestone in the area's industrial activity, which spans over 350 years. Rensselaer has been a crucial railroad hub on the continent, contributing significantly to its economic growth. The city is also home to the historic Crailo, a testament to its rich past.

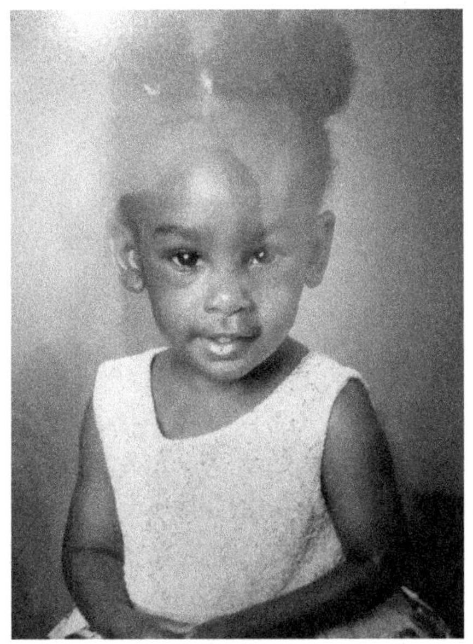

Picture of "Josie"

| 7 |

Josefina Catherine Cunningham

Josefina Catherine Cunninham known as "Josie" a three year old African American little girl who was raped and murdered by a white man named Robert Fisher in Rensselaer, New York. Born on

July 25, 2019 at St. Peter's Memorial Hospital in Albany, New York. Her parents were Lakeisha Stewart and Joseph Cunningham. Josie was sweet and innocent and had aspirations of becoming a firefighter from an early age. Her life, destined for historical significance, began at 1552 Broadway in Rensselaer, New York, where she was raised.

But In the summer of 2023 , Josefina was three years old and approaching her fourth birthday. When Josefina's brother, Jy'Quan, visited his mother's house, he noticed a white man with glasses sitting on the couch beside their mother, Lakeisha Stewart. Lakeisha initially introduced the man as a mechanic but later revealed him to be her new boyfriend. Josefina's mother, Lakeisha, had known Robert Fisher for only one week. A few days before her death Jy'Quan did stop by his mother's house to pick up keys and he saw his sister Josefina for the last time running around and playing with her toys. Jy'Quan took a lyft back to his home in Troy, New York. Later that evening Robert Fisher told Lakeisha "To go to the grocery store" and Josefina asked her mother if she could go with her. Her mother told her no.

Lakeisha then headed to the grocery store leaving Josefina alone with Fisher. When Lakeisha came back home she went to check on Josefina and she was sound asleep. Everything changed on the morning of July 7th 2023 when Lakeisha was waking Josefina up to bring her to daycare and found Josie dead covered in blue spots. Lakeisha called 911 and Fisher gave her a hug because she was crying and to cover up her murdered Josefina.

When police officer's came they told everyone to leave the house until the investigation was complete. Jy'Quan heard the news about Josefina's death from his aunt and immediately went to his mother's house upon arrival there yellow tape and police officers guarded outside the house. Shortly after the family went to the Albany Medical Center where Josefina was pronounced dead and Both Lakeisha and the brother Jy'Quan later found Josefina was drugged, murder and Raped Robert Fisher. The worse news was that he struck her to make her unconscious. Once the story about Josefina death was released to the public, local and regional press began picking up the story. A month later he pleaded not guilty at Rensselaer County Court in 2023 but a few months later Jy'Quan took matters in his own hand by using social media to reach out to the National Press about resignation of the New York State Death Penalty making this case a part of National African American history. Two weeks before his trial in 2024 Fisher pleaded guilty which sparked the interest of National News Outlets like NABJ, Black Enterprise, Atlanta Black Star, and The U.S Sun making the story historically significant.

www.ingramcontent.com/pod-product-compliance
Lightning Source LLC
Chambersburg PA
CBHW051410150726
48000CB00003B/1408